1   Introduction

Since the seminal work of Coase (1937), firms' organizational form decisions have preoccupied industrial economists.[1] Different theoretical perspectives on the boundaries of the firm have been advanced, and empirical researchers have credibly established that these theories have considerable explanatory power in a wide variety of settings.[2] By comparison, much less empirical evidence exists for the economic implications of organizational form decisions (Mullainathan and Scharfstein, 2001, Hubbard, 2008). This scarcity may seem surprising given that economic outcomes ultimately should be of primary importance. However, as Kosova et al. (2010) explain, the problem is not a lack of scholarly interest but that the choice of form and its economic implications are likely to be simultaneously determined. This makes it difficult to empirically identify the impact of organizational form separately from its determinants.

One common approach to dealing with the identification problem has been to seek out plausibly exogenous policy or other types of shocks that affect the contract choice set. Though they have been influential and informative, studies exploiting such shocks are subject to the critique that they identify the impact of sub-optimal choices. Thus, it is not surprising that scholars have generally found effects of substantial magnitude when employing this approach (Vita, 2000, Perez-Gonzalez, 2005). The marginal impact of variation in contract choice might well differ when firms are freely optimizing.

I examine these issues in the context of the gasoline industry. My study has two distinguishing elements. First, the empirical strategy is guided by a theoretical model of contract and price choice. The model is grounded in the institutional details of retail gasoline sales, and suggests that vertically separated stations should charge higher prices as a result of both effort-induced demand shifting and double marginalization. Moreover, it emphasizes the fundamental endogeneity of con-

---

[1] These issues should not simply interest academics, however. Lafontaine and Slade (2007) report that transactions in the market are approximately equalled by those performed within firms.

[2] E.g., agency theory (Holmstrom and Milgrom, 1991), transactions cost economics (Williamson, 1975), and the property rights theory of the firm (Grossman and Hart, 1986, Hart and Moore, 1990).

tract choice, while also pointing out that factors related to contractual complementarities will serve as instruments insofar as they do not separately impact economic behavior. In the model, such contractual complementarities arise from the principal's need to restrain agents' moral hazard, which is consistent with the existing literature (Klein, 1980, 1995, Brickley and Dark, 1987, Brickley, 1999). Second, the paper exploits a unique dataset that provides the organizational forms of gasoline stations, stations' brand affiliations, information on station characteristics (such as the presence of a convenience store or service bays), the prices of different types of gasoline being offered, and total volume of fuel sold. The comparative richness of these data makes it possible to investigate how variation in organizational form impacts economic behavior after taking account of the possible endogeneity of form choices.

Overall, the empirical analyses supports the theoretical model's prediction that vertically separated stations charge higher prices than do stations operated by salaried employees of large, vertically integrated gasoline refiners. The implied differences are of smaller but broadly similar magnitude to previous studies of this industry that exploit policy shocks to identify the impact of form (Vita, 2000). The difference in magnitude is consistent with the argument that identification from sweeping policy changes can overstate the marginal impact of form. In line with the findings about price, as well as the model's assumption of downward sloping demand, I also find lower sales volumes at the vertically separated stations. Moreover, I find statistically significant differences in the volume sold across the various vertically separated contracts, which suggests, first, that these stations' higher prices are attributable to both demand shifting and double-marginalization, and, second, that their relative roles differ across the vertically separated types. In particular, the data imply that the price increases at stations run by highly-incentivized local managers, but owned by refiners, may reflect greater demand shifting efforts relative to the other vertically separated contracts.

The paper contributes to a small but growing literature seeking to disentangle the determinants of organizational form from organizational form's impact on economic outcomes. In an early contribution, Masten et al. (1991) employed a structural approach to identify the impact of form on naval construction projects. They found that "incorrectly" choosing to integrate a project led organizational costs to increase by 70 percent, while an erroneous outsourcing decision trebled organizational costs. More recently, Novak and Stern (2008) and Forbes and Lederman (2010) use instrumental variables approaches based on complementarities in contracting forms to exogenously identify the impact of vertical integration. Both papers find that vertical separation has significant behavioral impacts on performance in the context of automobile manufacturing and air travel, respectively. Pursuing a similar identification strategy in a very different industry setting, Kosova et al. (2010) analyze the impact of vertical separation using data on a large hotel company's operations. Unlike the previous papers, they find that organizational form choice has a negligible impact upon economic outcomes after controlling for the choice of form. In other words, the company they study achieved very consistent results and behavior across affiliated units despite – or perhaps *through* – employing different vertical contracts. While I employ an instrumental variables approach similar to the one used in Kosova et al. (2010), my findings are closer to the pattern set by Masten et al. (1991), Novak and Stern (2008), and Forbes and Lederman (2010) insofar as I find sizable behavioral differences depending on the degree of vertical separation.

The paper proceeds as follows. In section 2, I review the theoretical perspectives on why vertical contracting might influence economic behavior, describe the institutional background of the retail gasoline industry, paying special attention to the different contractual forms employed, and quickly summarize the past evidence for organizational form's impact on behavior in this industry. In section 3, I develop a theoretical framework endogenizing the choice of both organizational form and price that is based on the multitask-agency model of contract choice of Slade (1996). Section 4 describes the data used in the analysis and presents preliminary evidence on the usage of different contractual forms and the behavioral variation across them. In section 5, I describe the econometric approach and results. Section 6 concludes and discusses possible extensions to the analysis.

4

2 Organizational Form, Economic Behavior, and Gasoline Retailing

2.1 Theoretical Perspectives

In the context of retail transactions, the economic literature relates the boundaries of the firm to economic behavior and performance primarily through two different channels: agency theory and double marginalization.[3]

Agency problems arise when costly employee effort affects profits, and employers cannot perfectly infer employee effort from observable information. Canonical agency theory (Holmstrom and Milgrom, 1991, Laffont and Martimort, 2002) has shown that a principal (i.e., the employer) facing this situation may be able to increase profits by offering "high powered" incentives that tie agents' (i.e., employees) compensation explicitly to one or more (generally output-related) performance metrics. In most retail settings, these contracts tend to be linear with the following form: $\beta q + \gamma$, where β represents a commission related to observable but stochastic metric q, and γ is a fixed payment.[4] If two contracts have the same expected value, then the one with the higher β should be considered higher-powered as it links pay more tightly to performance. The limiting cases are instructive. When $\beta = 0$, the agent is a salaried employee of the principal. If β is the retail margin, then the agent is the full residual claimant. In effect, the principal has "sold the firm" to the agent.

The viability of high-powered contracts crucially depends on factors like the observability of effort, the presence of other tasks, and the possibility of incentive conflicts across tasks. When high-powered contracts are efficient, the expected effect is to increase profits. However, the contracts' impact on other economic outcomes is unclear. For example, if higher effort on the part of the local agent reduces costs (Shelton, 1967), vertical separation as a result of higher-powered contracts,

---

[3]My treatment of the past literature is necessarily brief; however, more complete assessments are readily available. See, in particular, Lafontaine and Slade (2007, 2011).

[4]It is also worth noting that this formulation is consistent with traditional franchise contracting wherein the principal sells a good to the agent. By comparison, in business format franchising, the principal takes a cut of the agent's revenues. The linear model presented here could be straightforwardly changed to address this alternative situation.

could have no (or even a negative) effect on prices. On the other hand, if the agent's efforts raise demand, then prices might increase.

Double marginalization (Spengler, 1950), by contrast, has unambiguous behavioral implications. This theory shows that vertical separation – such as occurs with high-powered contracts – leads to higher prices than an integrated firm would choose when the upstream firm charges a wholesale price and the downstream entity has some degree of market power. These higher prices lead to lower aggregate profits than would be achieved by a vertically integrated firm.

The two stories presented above both take for granted that high-powered contracts are self-enforcing, and that there is no incentive conflict between the principal and agent beyond that relating to demand- (or cost-) shifting effort. In practice, however, this assumption often does not hold because of the impossibility of writing contracts that cause local agents' to fully internalize the effects of their actions on the principal, and the existence of multiple local margins impacting the principal's interests. If local agents benefit disproportionately from effort on some these margins, principals are vulnerable to moral hazard (Klein, 1980, 1995, Brickley and Dark, 1987, Brickley, 1999).

In an influential contribution to this literature, Brickley and Dark (1987) emphasize monitoring problems in the context of reputational consequences for branded retail chains, pointing out that when customers are unlikely to visit any given outlet again, a high-powered local manager may shirk on those elements that go to maintaining the overall brand's reputation. Consistent with this argument, Brickley and Dark (1987) showed that franchise contracts were less likely to be used in industries where the likelihood of non-repeat customers was high.

Beyond market isolation, scholars have considered other factors that will impact the desirability of different contract choices based on principals' ability to restrain their agents or other contract-related costs (Lafontaine and Slade, 1996, 2007, Novak and Stern, 2009, Kosova et al., 2010, Forbes and Lederman, 2009). The possibility of externalities from other contract choices is one such element. In the context of retail operations, externalities can easily be contemplated with respect to monitoring. If there is a chance that highly-incentivized local managers will behave in ways contrary to the principal's interests, then the principal will wish to check that they are not doing so. Thus, having outlets under similarly organized contracts nearby reduces the marginal cost of an additional outlet under that contract. This is because the principal already needs to devote resources to ensuring the nearby contracts are being appropriately honored, making the additional monitoring cost lower than if there were no other nearby outlets being monitored.

Thus, in aggregate, economic theory produces ambiguous predictions as to the relationship between the boundaries of the firm and economic behavior. However, greater precision can be made by exploiting institutional knowledge to gain insight into effort's impact. As a result, I now turn to an examination of the characteristics of vertical contracting in the retail gasoline sector.

2.2   Gasoline Retailing, Vertical Contracts, and Past Evidence

Gasoline stations can be divided into two categories. The first set includes those affiliated with refiners (e.g., Exxon or Shell), which accounted for 78% of the industry in 2002 (Kleit, 2005). The second set of stations are not tied to any particular refiner, and are commonly referred to as independents. Independents may purchase whatever brand of gasoline they choose, while those affiliated with refiners only use that refiner's gasoline. I focus on vertical contract choice at the refiner-affiliated stations, which are both more common and whose concerns connect especially straightforwardly to principal-agent models of vertical integration (Shepard, 1993, Slade, 1996).

In general, the refiner sets the terms of the contracts, allowing it to best respond to variation in both market and station characteristics. Such variation can be quite pronounced because while gasoline stations' core product is fairly homogeneous, they are horizontally differentiated competitors that compete on price, location, and non-gasoline "quality" (e.g., service or station cleanliness). In addition, stations differentiate themselves using the presence and pricing of alternative services (e.g., convenience store or repairs).[5] Different combinations of station and market characteristics

---

[5]See Kleit (2005) or Hosken et al. (2008) for surveys of retail gasoline markets.

make different organizational forms more (less) desirable. While form decisions can be updated, it is rare for station – as opposed to market – characteristics to change over time.[6]

The data I use were compiled by New Image Marketing – a consulting company, which divides stations into four mutually exclusive modes of ownership.[7] While precise contractual details for the different forms are unavailable from New Image, the categories broadly correspond to forms examined elsewhere in the literature on gasoline retailing (Shepard, 1993, Slade, 1996, Meyer and Fischer, 2004, Kleit, 2005). The contract types are described below.

Salary Operation Under salaried contracts, the station and the land on which it sits are wholly-owned by the refiners, and all station personnel are salaried refiner employees. This form corresponds to contracts that allocate all decision-making authority to the principal, and closely resemble company-owned, "low-powered" contracts that are common in other retail industries, including fast food and lodging. While there may be occasional intra-firm tournaments designed to induce extra effort from employees, the station personnel never have control over gasoline pricing. Thus, $\beta = 0$ and $\gamma > 0$ for this contract type.

Lessee Dealer As with salaried stations, the vertically integrated refiners continue to own the land and building under lessee dealer contracts. However, instead of using salaried employees, refiners lease the station to local entrepreneurs, known as lessee dealers, who also purchase gasoline from them at a price set by the refiner. This price is typically referred to as the dealer tank wagon (DTW) price, which is the same for all lessee dealers within a narrow geographic region, known as a price zone, but can vary across zones.[8] Unlike salaried stations, lessee dealers set prices for gasoline (and any other goods available at the station) and, importantly, pursue promotions designed to foster local demand.[9] Such promotions might include linkages to other local businesses or the provision of specific, locally valued services. Anecdotally, there is some evidence that lessee

---

[6]For example, in the data used in the analysis, the coefficient of variation for the dummy indicating the presence of service bays is less than 0.18.

[7]The precise definitions used by New Image are shown in Appendix B.

[8]See Meyer and Fischer (2004) for consideration of the economic impact of price zones.

[9]Because the principal retains an ownership stake but relinquishes control to outside parties, this form is thus the opposite of the "management contract" form observed in lodging. For details on different incentives for control and ownership in an international context, see Lafontaine et al. (2011).

dealers charge higher prices than salaried operations. For example, Kleit (2005, pp. 10-11) notes that Senator Carl Levin stated that his staff heard stories that lessee dealers were warned that if they charged higher prices, then their DTW price would be increased as punishment. Overall, these characteristics indicate that $0 < \beta$ and $0 > \gamma$ for this contract.

Open Dealer Open dealer contracts closely resemble lessee dealer contracts except that the local agent owns the land and station. Previous research has found that open dealer stations tend to be rare in urban areas and more common in rural regions. This may reflect the fact that it is easier for a refiner to determine good locations to build stations in densely populated areas than in rural ones. As with lessee dealer stations, one of the advantages of using an open dealer format is that local agents are incentivized to promote demand through the most effective channels available to them. In terms of the supply of gasoline, open dealers may procure their gasoline from the refiner as lessee dealers do. However, as noted in Meyer and Fischer (2004), they also commonly purchase their gasoline from a wholesaler who has purchased gasoline from the refiner, who purchase gasoline from the refiner and then pick the price at which they sell to stations. Overall, these results can be summarized as $0 < \beta$ and $0 = \gamma$.

Jobber/Wholesaler The final contract category is identical to open dealer but for the fact that the owner of the land and station owns multiple stations.[10] The owners are often branded convenience store chains or jobbers. Overall, $0 < \beta$ and $0 = \gamma$ for this contract.

Unfortunately, it is difficult to hypothesize about how to compare the βs for the different vertically separated forms. While one might think that lessee dealer contracts should be higher powered than the others since they must pay rent to the refiner, industry anecdotes suggest that at least in some cases refiners charge below market rents to lessee dealers. This would suggest that β could in fact be lower than for the other forms. Similarly, it is difficult to know how to think of local incentives for jobber-owned stations, who might have more bargaining power over β but have reduced station-level incentives. Overall, I leave the relative orderings of the different forms

---

[10]Thus, these agents resemble the multi-franchise companies that are common in other franchising industries (Kalnins and Lafontaine, 2004).

as something to be considered empirically.

2.3   Past Evidence of the Impact of Form in Gasoline Retailing

The gasoline industry has long attracted attention from scholars seeking to understand the implications of contractual variation. Researchers chiefly have focused on the unambiguous prediction provided by the theory of double marginalization. In order to account for the (likely) endogeneity of form choices, many authors have exploited divorcement laws, which restrict the utilization of vertically integrated contracts. Using state-level data on gasoline prices and instrumenting for the choice to adopt divorcement laws, Vita (2000) showed that states with divorcement laws did indeed have higher prices. Similarly, Barron and Umbeck (1984) found that gasoline stations that switched to vertically separated contracts after a divestiture law in Maryland had higher prices.

While influential and convincing in the manner in which they deal with the endogeneity of form, these papers rely on policy changes that dramatically raise the costs (to infinity in some cases) of using vertically integrated contracts. They thus are likely to be identifying the impact of form off of inframarginal as well as marginal stations, which makes it unsurprising that they find economically and statistically significant effects.

Consistent with this critique, studies exploiting identification strategies other than policy changes, have found more ambiguous relationships between vertical separation and performance. For example, identifying off of a merger, Hastings (2004) found no effect from vertical separation.[11] Controlling for market and brand effects, Shepard (1993) found only limited evidence consistent with double marginalization, while Hosken et al. (2008) found some evidence correlating company owned and operated (i.e., vertically integrated) stations with *higher* prices.

Thus, the relationship between form and economic behavior remains an open question even in the oft-studied retail gasoline industry.

---

[11]Taylor et al. (2010) present evidence that the data used by Hastings may have been problematic.

3   Multitask Model of Gasoline Retailing

To gain insight into the relationship between form choice and pricing, I build on the multitask principal-agent model of Slade (1996), which incorporated price-setting into the canonical work of Holmstrom and Milgrom (1991). In the model, the agent has up to two tasks, at least one of which is selling gasoline. The other might be repairing cars or running a convenience store.[12] Assuming a linear demand curve, the model relates local effort, output, and price in the following manner:

$$q = a - Bp + e + \epsilon, \ \epsilon \sim N(0, \Sigma), \ \Sigma = (\sigma_{ij}), \tag{1}$$

where q, p, and e are the output, price, and effort vectors. Demand is characterized by the vector a and matrix B, and ϵ is a vector of random shocks drawn from a bivariate-normal distribution. B is assumed to be a symmetric, positive definite matrix, and the off-diagonal term b_{ij} indicates the extent of demand complementarity for the output from the two different tasks. Similarly, the off-diagonal term σ_{ij} of Σ captures the degree to which shocks to the different tasks are correlated. The diagonal terms σ_{ii} indicate the difficulty the principal has in inferring the agent's level of effort from the observed output.

The formulation of demand shown in Equation 1 imposes that the effort of local agents affects profits by shifting the demand curve. As discussed above, this is consistent with the institutional details of the gasoline retailing industry, in which highly-incentivized local agents are generally placed in charge of promotions (Kleit, 2005).

Assuming that the marginal cost of upstream production is zero, the risk-neutral principal's profit, π, will be the difference between downstream revenues and managerial costs. I assume that these costs can be divided into two segments. The first consists of the net compensation paid to the agent, y. Assuming that y has the linear form $\beta q + \gamma$ and the agent's cost of effort is quadratic,

---

[12]Note that the model could easily be generalized to three or more tasks. Also, the qualitative implications are consistent if we assume that the second task is along the lines of maintenance quality. This would give it a flavor somewhat similar to that of Lafontaine and Slade (1996).

the agent's income can be expressed as:

$$y = \beta'q + \gamma - \frac{e'Ce}{2}. \tag{2}$$

Making the standard assumption that the agent has a negative-binomial utility function with coefficient of absolute-risk aversion r (i.e., $u(y) = -\exp(-ry)$) means that the agent's certainty equivalent (CE) income is:

$$
\begin{aligned}
CE &= E(y) - \frac{r}{2}Var(y) \\
&= \beta'(a - Bp + e) + \gamma - \frac{e'Ce}{2} - \frac{r}{2}\beta'\Sigma\beta. \tag{3}
\end{aligned}
$$

The second element of managerial costs are those related to monitoring the local agent's behavior, $M(\beta, Z)$. In the context of gasoline retailing, monitoring is necessary to ensure that local stations maintain appropriate levels of cleanliness, etc., which a highly incentivized local agent might prefer to shirk on in order to devote more effort to increasing sales. I assume that the principal's monitoring costs are an increasing, non-negative function of β and are also influenced by one or more elements Z, which are unrelated to local demand conditions or the agent's cost of effort. I also assume that $M(0, Z) = 0$ for all Z. In other words, in vertically integrated contracts, the principal has no monitoring costs.

The game between the principal and agent proceeds sequentially. First, the principal chooses the terms of the contract (β, γ), and offers it to the agent on a take-it-or-leave-it basis. If the agent accepts the offer, she then chooses effort e. Making the standard assumption that the contracts are efficient and that the principal uses the fixed fee γ to divide up surplus, the principal's problem is:

$$\max_{\beta, p, e} p'(a - Bp + e) - \frac{e'Ce}{2} - \frac{r}{2}\beta'\Sigma\beta - M(\beta, Z), \tag{4}$$

subject to the agent's incentive-compatibility constraint of:

$$e = \mathrm{argmax} \left(\beta'(a - Bp + e) - \frac{e'Ce}{2} \right). \tag{5}$$

The first-order condition for the agent is $\beta - Ce = 0$, which leads to optimal effort $e^* = C^{-1}\beta$. Thus, Equation (4) can be rewritten as the unconstrained maximization problem:

$$\max_{\beta,p} p'(a - Bp + C^{-1}\beta) - \frac{\beta'C\beta}{2} - \frac{r}{2}\beta'\Sigma\beta - M(\beta, Z). \tag{6}$$

Assuming an interior solution for effort (i.e., $e^* > 0$), the FOC for β and p are $C^{-1}p - C^{-1}\beta - r\Sigma\beta = 0$ and $a - 2Bp + C^{-1}\beta = 0$, respectively. Combining these two equations and solving for β yields the optimal contract:

$$\beta^* = (2CB(I + rC\Sigma) - I)^{-1}(Ca - 2CBC\ M_\beta(Z)), \tag{7}$$

where $M_\beta(Z)$ is the non-negative first derivative of M with respect to β.

Rearranging the FOC for β yields $p = (I + rC\Sigma)\beta$. Substituting in Equation 7 produces the optimal price as a function of the environment:

$$p^* = (I + rC\Sigma)(2CB(I + rC\Sigma) - I)^{-1}(Ca - 2CBC\ M_\beta(Z)). \tag{8}$$

As the optimal β must necessarily be positive, this expression implies that greater vertical separation should be associated with higher prices. Unfortunately, however, Equations 7 and 8 are not very transparent as to why separation leads to this result nor the relationship between station environment and pricing. Greater clarity into these issues can be gained by making a number of assumptions. First, following Slade (1996) and consistent with the institutional characteristics of gasoline retailing, I make the assumption that the market price of the second activity (if there is one) is determined by local market conditions and is thus not part of the choice set.[13] Second, arms-length contracts in the retail gasoline industry usually proceed as follows: the principal sells gasoline to the agent at some wholesale price, and the agent then chooses the retail price. Thus, we can re-express agents' variable wages as $\beta = p_1 - \alpha$, where α is the wholesale price that the agent paid. Third, in practice, principals' set of available organizational forms are rarely continuous. Instead, firms must select from a set of predetermined contracts.[14] Moreover, the levels of β in the predetermined contracts tend to be closely correlated. In other words, if an agent is given high-powered incentives for one task, they will be given high powered incentives in the other.

These restrictions transform the principal's contract decision into a recursive discrete choice problem. The principal must consider the agent's behavior under the different possible contracts – conditional on the environment in which the contract will be performed – and then select the contract form that will lead to highest profits. Insight into how contract choice as well as the other model parameters impact pricing can be gained by focusing on specific contract cases.

Case 1: Complete Integration. Assume that the principal decides to use a vertically integrated contract, and that the price of the second activity is exogenously determined by market conditions. Insofar as I specified that monitoring costs are 0 under vertical integration, this means that Equation 6 simplifies to:

$$\pi^{I*} = \max_{p_1} p_1(a_1 - b_{11}p_1 - b_{12}p_2) + p_2(a_2 - b_{12}p_1 - b_{22}p_2), \tag{9}$$

while the optimal price becomes:

$$p_1^{I*} = \frac{a_1 - 2b_{12}p_2}{2b_{11}}, \tag{10}$$

where the superscript identifies the special case.

---

[13]This assumption is also consistent with the model of Lal and Matutes (1994), wherein imperfectly informed consumers make decisions about which multi-product retailer to frequent based on the advertised price of one good.
[14]See discussion in Blair and Lafontaine (2005).

14

Case 2: Partial Separation. Now assume that the principal makes the agent the full residual claimant for the second activity, whose price remains exogenously determined. The principal also gives high-powered gasoline-selling incentives to the agent by making them the full residual claimant after the payment of predetermined wholesale price α.[15] Since the usage of a high-powered contract means that the principal now must monitor the agent's behavior, this means that Equation 6 becomes:

$$\pi^{S*} = \max_{p_1} p_1(a_1 - b_{11}p_1 - b_{12}p_2 + \tilde{c_{11}}(p_1 - \alpha) + \tilde{c_{12}}p_2) + p_2(a_2 + b_{12}p_1$$

$$+b_{22}p_2 + \tilde{c_{12}}(p_1 - \alpha) + \tilde{c_{22}}p_2) - \tfrac{1}{2}(\tilde{c_{11}}(p_1^2 - 2p_1\alpha + \alpha^2) + 2\tilde{c_{12}}(p_1 - \alpha)p_2 + \tilde{c_{22}}p_2^2)$$

$$-\tfrac{r}{2}(\sigma_{11}(p_1^2 - 2p_1\alpha + \alpha^2) + 2\sigma_{12}(p_1 - \alpha)p_2 + \sigma_{22}p_2^2) - M(\alpha, Z), \tag{11}$$

where $\tilde{C} = (\tilde{c_{ij}}) = C^{-1}$. This leads to the optimal price function:

$$p_1^{S*} = \frac{a_1 - p_2(2b_{12} - \tilde{c_{12}} + r\sigma_{12}) + \sigma_{11}r\alpha}{2b_{11} - \tilde{c_{11}} + r\sigma_{11}}. \tag{12}$$

It is important to note that since monitoring costs are not a function of local market price, and contract choice is predetermined, the optimal price even under a vertically separated contract is not affected by M once the contract has been chosen. In other words, monitoring costs have no impact on pricing save through the choice of contract.

Intuitively, the optimal prices expressed in Equations 10 and 12 bear strong similarities to each other. A key implication of both is that multi-product stations are likely to charge lower prices for gasoline than those stations that focus just on gasoline retailing. Moreover, as the price of the second good increases, the price for the first good should fall. Similarly, as demand complementarity b_{12} increases, p_1 should decline. All of these results stem from the fact that the station can take advantage of demand complementarities to raise profits by selling the second good (if it exists) to consumers attracted to the low prices of the first.

---

[15]The predetermined nature of α stems in part from importance of price zones.

Comparing Equations 10 and 12, as well as Equations 9 and 11, also yields insight into how variation in organizational form translates to behavioral differences. These insights can be summarized as follows.

PROPOSITION 1: *Conditional on an arms-length contractual form being chosen in equilibrium for a station, its prices will on average be higher than if it was operated as a salaried operation.*

PROOF: All proofs in Appendix A.

Consistent with the general intuition provided by Equation 8, Proposition 1 states that prices will be higher at stations operated under arms-length contracts conditional on the principal choosing to use an arms-length contract. The intuition for the proof is straightforward. The only reason to use a vertically separated contract is to motivate the agent to increase demand by exerting greater effort. As shown in Equation (1), this linearly shifts the demand curve out, increasing price.

COROLLARY 1: *The price increase caused by vertical separation can be decomposed into two separate influences: i) Double marginalization; and ii) Demand-shifting. Moreover, even in the absence of double-marginalization, the demand-shifting effect will lead – on average – to higher prices at stations operated under high-powered contracts.*

Corollary 1 indicates that the higher prices at vertically separated stations is due to two distinct effects. Equation 12 shows that the term with α enters additively. This term thus directly captures the impact of double marginalization, which is driven by the wholesale price charged by the refiner. As the wholesale price α increases, the retail price at stations using arms length contracts linearly increases.

The second reason for higher prices at vertically separated stations is due to demand-shifting. As stated in Corollary 1, a vertically-separated station will charge a higher price for gasoline even if $\alpha = 0$. This is because the local agent's efforts cause demand to shift out. The magnitude of the demand-shifting term is driven by several different model parameters. In particular, as effort becomes costlier, either for gasoline retailing or in its impact on effort elsewhere, then the increase in price from switching to an arms length contract increases. If we assume – as seems reasonable

16

– that it is more costly to switch from selling gasoline to repairing cars than from selling gasoline to selling convenience store items, then this suggests that the price of gasoline should be higher in stations with repair bays than ones with convenience stores, all else equal. Uncertainty – and the agents' tastes for it – also prominently impacts the effort-shifting gap. When demand shocks for the two services are more correlated, the magnitude of the effort-induced price gap falls as agents have less incentive to work hard since their payoffs are less certain. Relatedly, as agents' risk aversion increases, the price gap falls as their effort decreases.

PROPOSITION 2: *The factors that lead to a larger demand-shifting effect on prices also increase the desirability of using an arms-length contract.*

Proposition 2 implies that unconditional examinations of pricing differences will overstate the true magnitude of vertical separations's marginal impact on retail pricing. This occurs because there may be regions where, in equilibrium, one form or the other is clearly preferred due to the demand-shifting effect, which increases both profits and prices at vertically separated stations. However, Proposition 2 does not contradict the finding in Proposition 1 that we should expect to see a difference in pricing – even when the wholesale cost does not include a markup over the principals' marginal cost. Instead, the Proposition emphasizes the importance of controlling for the selection of form before estimating the impact of form on economic behavior. The model suggests a way around this difficulty. Insofar as the underlying drivers of monitoring costs, Z, are unrelated to the agent's behavior, they can act as instruments in regressions of economic outcomes on contract choice. Below, I exploit this implication to test the predictions highlighted by the two Propositions.

4 Data

As noted above, my principal sources of data are regional censuses of retail gasoline stations assembled by New Image Marketing. The data were collected in person by New Image employees, who assessed different visually observable station characteristics before talking with on-site staff about ownership and other factors. Stations are uniquely identified by location code within states.

The New Image data contain information on the operations and organization of refiner-affiliated stations as well as "independent" stations.

Restricting the sample to stations affiliated with refiners leaves 4687 station-period observations affiliated with 3677 different unique station locations.[16] Although not common, some locations do change brands during the sample period. These changes appear unrelated to changes in organizational form.[17]

As previously noted, the operations surveyed are in the Denver, Minneapolis, Toledo, Louisville, and Washington, DC metro areas, and were collected at uneven intervals between 1996 and 1999. Observations are not evenly distributed across time periods or states. Table C-1 shows the number of observations by state and year. Consistent with the fact that the different states have different laws affecting refiners' ability to own and operate stations, the relative usage of the organizational forms in the different market areas varies significantly. This can be seen in Table C-2.[18] Pooling the observations, the Table shows that the different contractual types account for 13%, 40%, 24% and 23% of the sample, respectively. The share of stations operated directly by refiners is consistent with the estimated national average of 10-20% cited in Kleit (2005).

I analyze economic behavior by exploiting the listed prices of regular, super (i.e., medium), and premium quality gasolines, as well as the volume that the station employee reported being sold in the preceding month. Some caution must be attached to the final variable, however, as it relates to the *total* volume sold without regard to grade or even whether the fuel was diesel or gasoline. The inability to distinguish the volumes sold of the different types of fuel makes it difficult to present revenue results as done in Kosova et al. (2010).[19]

---

[16]The retail chains included in the branded sample are: Amoco, Ashland, BP, Chevron, Citgo, Conoco, Crown, Exxon, Marathon, Mobil, Phillips, Shamrock, Shell, Sinclair, Speedway, Sunoco, Super America, Texaco, and Total.

[17]Because of the infrequency of changes in form, I am hesitant to employ fixed effects models that identify the impact of contract based solely on within-station changes. However, preliminary analyses were consistent in sign and magnitude with those presented below though sensitive to the inclusion of different controls.

[18]Virginia, Maryland, and the District of Columbia all have divorcement laws. As noted above, these laws limit (or prohibit) use of salaried operations. The strength of these laws varies across the different states, with those of Maryland and DC being much stronger than that of Virginia.

[19]Exploratory analyses that use a revenue proxy generated by multiplying regular price by volume indicate that the vertically separated stations have lower revenues, especially the open dealer and jobber-owned stations. This is consistent with the findings about demand-shifting relative to double marginalization under the different contracts

Besides branding, the New Image data provide information on a large number of different exogenous and endogenous station features. These characteristics include the presence of a convenience store, the number of service bays, and the appearance of the station, and are used as controls in my analyses. In addition, I proxy for the intensity of local competition using the number of stations in the zipcode.[20] To supplement the station censuses, I obtain county population data from the U.S. Census and average household income (in thousands) taken from the Statistics of Income (SOI) collected by the Internal Revenue Service to further account for market variation.[21] I show descriptive statistics for all observations in Table 1.

Table 2 compares the summary statistics between vertically separated and vertically integrated stations, and indicates significant differences across them. As predicted by the model presented above, the unconditional prices charged in salaried stations are much lower. The data also show that salaried stations sell larger volumes of gasoline. The null hypotheses that these behavioral differences are statistically indistinguishable from 0 are strongly rejected. Interestingly, the data also show behavioral differences across the vertically separated forms, which can be seen in Table 3. Although more modest in magnitude, the differences are also statistically significant at conventional levels; lessee dealer stations both price more highly and sell larger volumes than the other forms. This may suggest that the relative intensity of incentives varies across the different forms, a possibility about which the theoretical model was agnostic.

However, in addition to suggesting differences in economic behavior across contracts, Tables 2 and 3 also highlight differences across contract types. First, stations operated by open dealers are substantially less likely to include convenience stores, which is in-line with previous findings (Shepard, 1993). Second, open-dealer and lessee-dealer stations are much more likely to have repair operations than either company- or jobber- owned stations, which also is consistent with the pre-

---

discussed below. Details are available upon request.

[20]The precise definitions for the New Image controls are given in Appendix B as well as how they were transformed for use in the econometric analysis. In addition, I generated qualitatively similar results using the New Image variable capturing the number of branded competitors visible from the station instead of the number of stations in the zipcode.

[21]See http://www.census.gov/popest/counties/ and http://www.irs.gov/taxstats/article/0,,id=120303,00.html, respectively.

vious literature (Shepard, 1993, Slade, 1996, Blass and Carlton, 2001). Third, the Table indicates that the stations run by salaried employees of the refiner are notably more attractive in appearance. This is in line with the findings of Michael (2000) and Jin and Leslie (2009) in other industries. Fourth, all of the vertically separated forms – especially the open dealer- and jobber-owned stations – are located in areas with lower income. Along similar lines, Slade (1996) found that forms with no refiner ownership stake are mainly utilized in rural communities.

Though the aggregate data patterns presented here suggest differences in economic behavior across forms, they also indicate consistent selection of different forms in different areas or situations. Thus, it is difficult to say with confidence whether the variation in pricing and sales volume can be attributed to differences in form as opposed to station and market characteristics. To obtain a more precise understanding of how contract type affects behavior, it is necessary to move to a formal econometric framework. In the next section, I use methods that exploit both within- and between-station variation, as well as plausibly exogenous differences in monitoring costs, in order to separately identify the impact of station characteristics and the impact of vertical separation.

5 Methodology and Results

5.1 Econometric Approach and Identification

My goal is to estimate the impact of organizational form on the behavior of gasoline stations. I focus on four different outcome variables: the prices of regular, super, and premium gasoline, and the total volume of fuel sold. I now discuss the econometric approaches I employ in testing how these factors are affected by organizational form.

All of my estimating equations are variants of the following linearly separable general form:

$$Y_{it} = F_{it}\delta + X_{it}\lambda + Z_i\nu + u_{it},$$

(13)

where i and t index stations and time of observation, respectively. Y is the economic outcome of

20

interest; F_{it} indicates the organizational form of station i in time t; X_{it} are time-varying station and market characteristics; Z_i are time-invariant station characteristics; and u_{it} is information unobservable to the econometrician. As in Vita (2000) and Hosken et al. (2008), I estimate the models in levels. However, the results are qualitatively identical when I employ a log-linear specification. Details are available upon request.

In addition to those observable explanatory variables discussed in the previous section, all regressions include brand and state-date indicator variables. These take account of systematic variation across chains, regions, and time periods, which is necessary as previous research has shown that different chains consistently price differently (Hosken et al., 2008). Moreover, the existence and severity of divorcement laws varies across the sample regions (Vita, 2000, Blass and Carlton, 2001). Similarly, within a given year, prices at different stations were collected at different times. However, within a region, prices were collected at similar times. By including state-date dummy variables, I ensure that my estimates are based off of variation within date and region, avoiding the possibility of confusing the impact of form with temporally or regulatorily driven differences.[22]

I assume that the unobserved information is a composite term, i.e., $u_{it} = \mu_i + \epsilon_{it}$, where μ_i represents station-specific heterogeneity and ϵ_{it} is the idiosyncratic error. Depending on μ's correlation with the explanatory variables, Equation 13 should be estimated in different ways. I employ different methods corresponding to different assumptions about the relationship between μ_i and the observable controls.

First, I make the strong assumption that the station-specific heterogeneity is uncorrelated with the other explanatory variables. In particular, this modeling approach effectively assumes that all monitoring characteristics are captured in the observables, including the region-date controls. To account for possible correlations over time and region, I cluster the standard errors at the zipcode level, which will allow for the possibility that stations close to each other may be subject to the same unobserved factors.

---

[22] The results are qualitatively similar when I include more and less parsimonious sets of controls. In particular, switching to county-date variables does not change the results. Details are available upon request.

The assumption of independence between the unobserved and observed factors required for the cross-sectional models is very strong. It is intuitive to think that some element of unobserved heterogeneity not picked up by the explanatory variables (e.g., managerial talent or demand conditions) is correlated with organizational form. If this is true, then the cross-sectional estimates suffer from omitted-variable bias. My second estimating approach addresses the possibility of correlation between the persistent unobserved information and the observable regressors by following Kosova et al. (2010) in specifying that the correlation can be captured through the inclusion of the station-level means of the time-varying regressors. This method stems from Mundlak (1978), who noted that the results from standard linear fixed effects (FE) models can be obtained in a random effects (RE) model if the means of time-varying regressors are included. In other words, I assume that:

$$\mu_i = \bar{X}_i \xi + \upsilon_i, \tag{14}$$

where $\bar{X}_i$ is the vector of station-level means of time-varying regressors, and υ_i represents time invariant station information that is uncorrelated with the observables.

Unfortunately, there are very few time-varying elements in my data as the station characteristics are largely fixed. For this reason, along with the means of county population and income, as well as the mean number of stations in the zipcode, I follow Kosova et al. (2010) and include the mean lagged volume (price) in the price (volume) regressions as well as the one-period lagged terms directly. These lagged terms can reasonably be thought to be exogenous at the time the decision-maker sets prices or the consumer determines where to purchase their gasoline. While these lagged terms help control for unobserved heterogeneity, they also mean that only stations with multiple observations are in the sample. Thus, all stations in MN, OH, and CO are dropped for these models.

Using the Mundlak approach, υ_i can be modeled in a variety of ways. I assume that the unobservable station-specific heterogeneity can be addressed by allowing the standard errors to be clustered at the station level. This allows for a more general correlation structure than RE, and hence is a conservative approach.[23]

While the Mundlak models do control for a considerable degree of heterogeneity, they continue to assume that monitoring issues are wholly captured via the included controls, which now include lags and the means of the time-varying elements. One might reasonably be concerned that the models are still fundamentally failing to account for the endogeneity of contract choice if there were a correlation between the idiosyncratic shocks, ϵ_{it}, and the choice of organizational forms. For example, the principals might prefer to keep stations under salaried managers in particularly attractive markets. Thus, a positive shock to demand would be correlated with a higher incidence of company-ownership, which would negatively bias the estimated effect of vertical separation.

I address concerns about these types of correlations using an instrumental variable approach that follows the implications of the theoretical model. Like other recent papers investigating the behavioral implications of contract type, I exploit the existence of complementarities in contract form choice to find instruments that will influence the selection of form but have no separate influence on economic behavior.[24] Consistent with the theoretical model's predictions, I follow Kosova et al. (2010) and focus on refiners' incentive to account for their own monitoring costs as well as product market behavior when selecting contract forms. I do this using the shares of nearby stations affiliated with a given brand in a given county organized under the different forms as instruments for the choice of form for each local operation.

As suggested above, the general idea for this instrumental variable approach is that having a large existing base of outlets under one contract lowers the marginal monitoring cost of an additional station. Wilson (2011) tests this theory explicitly using the same New Image data, and shows that the share of separated stations in the county has a major influence on whether or not an outlet

---

[23] In practice, the choice between clustering and RE has almost no effect on the estimates or their statistical significance. Details are available upon request.

[24] See Lafontaine and Slade (2007) for a review of the monitoring literature, with a special emphasis on franchising. Novak and Stern (2009) and Forbes and Lederman (2009) provide separate descriptions of how contracting complementarities arise in automobile manufacturing and air travel, which are used to identify instruments in their related papers.

is vertically separated. In addition to the contract share variables, in the pricing models, I also include the number of gasoline nozzles as an instrument. The past contracting literature surveyed in Lafontaine and Slade (2007) has shown that outlet size tends to be correlated with company operations, and there is no direct reason to assume that the number of pumps should have a separate impact upon demand or pricing. Obviously, this element cannot be included as an instrument in the volume models as it directly affects overall sales and is therefore employed as a regressor in those models.

I focus on the number of affiliated outlets in the county as opposed to zipcode, because I believe that conditional on traveling from their headquarters to a given county, it costs salaried employees of the principals little to travel between zipcodes to monitor different stations. Consistent with this argument, my results are qualitatively similar when I focus on brands' shares at the zipcode level. The estimated coefficients from the models using zipcodes are generally larger in magnitude but are no longer statistically significant at conventional levels. Given that brands frequently do not have more than one outlet in a zipcode, many observations are lost, making the lack of statistical significance unsurprising.

As noted in Wooldridge (2002), instrumental variables models can consistently be estimated using standard two-stage least squares. I estimate two variants corresponding to the pooled and Mundlak approaches described above.

5.2 Price Results

I present the price results in three separate tables, one for each grade of fuel. Tables 4, 5, and 6 show the results for regular, super, and premium quality gasolines, respectively. In each, the first four columns simply look at differences between vertically integrated and vertically separated stations as in Shepard (1993). Column 1 shows the result of the cross-sectional model, which does not account for possible correlations between any of the unobservable information and the choice of form. Column 2 shows the results of the Mundlak model, which controls for persistent unobserved heterogeneity using the means of the time-varying elements plus the lag of volume sold. Column 3 returns to the cross-sectional approach to dealing with station-level heterogeneity, but accounts for the endogeneity of form using the instrumental variable approach described above. Finally, Column 4 applies the instrumental variable approach to the Mundlak model. Columns 5 through 8 take analogous estimating approaches, but allow for different behavioral effects across the different types of organizational forms.

Overall, the results in Tables 4, 5, and 6 are quite consistent with the theoretical model's predictions, and show the importance of controlling for both unobserved time-invariant station characteristics and the endogeneity of form choice. In all twelve of the models using an indicator variable for whether a station is vertically separated or not, the estimated coefficient is positive. In the cross-sectional models, these effects are of small magnitude and are not statistically significant at conventional levels. However, they increase by more than an order of magnitude and substantial precision as I account for time-invariant heterogeneity and/or possible correlations between the unobserved information and form choice. Given their theoretical appeal, I much prefer these models, especially the one that addresses persistent heterogeneity as well as contemporaneous correlations between form and the unobserved information.[25]

The pattern seen for the models using a dichotomous contracting variable is largely repeated when I allow for different economic effects across the different contract types, and the magnitudes on the different forms are quite similar to those found for the simple "vertically separated" indicator model. In the cross-sectional models, I do not necessarily find positive, much less statistically significant, effects for all of the different contracts. However, accounting for persistent station-level heterogeneity leads to positive and statistically significant effects in almost every instance. Shifting to an instrumental variables approach tends to increase the magnitudes further, especially when I continue to account for the time-invariant heterogeneity.

---

[25]This belief is buttressed by C tests of the endogenous variables in the regressions on regular price. Insofar as all endogenous regressors were simultaneously considered, the tests are equivalent to Hausman tests comparing an OLS model to the IV model. The results strongly support the use of instrumental variables as opposed to OLS except in the case of the Mundlak model with individual dummies for each contract type.

Interestingly, the estimated effects for the different forms are never statistically distinguishable from each other when I employ the Mundlak approach. This indicates that conditional on deciding not to own and operate a station with its own employees, the refiner achieves consistent results despite using different contractual forms. It also suggests that it is appropriate to rely on the simple, dichotomous indicator variable model results, as they are more efficient.

Using the estimates recovered in Column 4 in the different Tables shows that vertical separation leads to price increases of 5 to 8 cents. Consistent with Proposition 2 of the theoretical model, which predicted that the market and station characteristics where arms-length organizational forms were used would compound the pricing gap, these differences are markedly less than the differences in sample means displayed in Table 2. It is interesting to compare the estimate for regular unleaded gasoline to that of Vita (2000), who found that, on average, states with divorcement laws had regular unleaded gas prices 2.6 cents higher than those without. Insofar as around 20% (or fewer) of stations are company-owned, my results would have predicted broadly comparable but slightly lower overall differences. This smaller estimate of the marginal impact of vertical separation is consistent with the argument that identification based on sweeping policy changes are capturing infra-marginal as well as changes on the margin, and thus may overstate the marginal impact of contractual change.

Notwithstanding their small magnitude, the models' coefficient estimates are of large economic significance. This is because gasoline retailing is a low margin and high volume industry. Thus, as discussed in Hosken et al. (2008) and Vita (2000), even modest changes in price levels can lead to sizable changes in the size and distribution of total welfare. Indeed, Hosken et al. (2008) and Kleit (2005) report that retail margins average 20 cents or less, indicating that the choice of form can change margins by 25 to 40%. However, despite the sizable magnitude of price increases due to vertical separation, it is not clear just how much consumer welfare would be lost by prohibiting salaried operations. This is because the model predicts that the price increase stems both from demand-shifting and the inefficiency of double marginalization. Without being able to separate the two, it is impossible to quantify the welfare effects on consumers.

Though not necessarily statistically significant at conventional levels, the results for the control variables reported in Tables 4, 5, and 6 also are broadly in line with the model's predictions and the prior literature. Consistent with intuition about the role of local competition, I find that the number of nearby stations likely exerts downward pressure on price (though this effect is not always of statistical or economic significance, especially when time-invariant station-level heterogeneity is accounted for). The model predicts that the presence of products with strong demand complementarities to gasoline should exert downward pressure on gasoline prices. This is consistent with the finding that the presence of a convenience store is negatively correlated with gasoline price. As in Slade (1996), I find that service capabilities – which might reasonably be thought to be inversely correlated with gasoline demand – are associated with higher prices. Interestingly, I find that stations with higher quality appearances tend to have lower prices, which may suggest cost complementarities between the provision of quality and other desired services. Finally, higher average household incomes are associated with higher prices. By contrast, population's impact is often negligible and inconsistently signed.

Overall, the results of the price regressions strongly support the two Propositions of the theoretical model. Vertically separated stations consistently charge higher prices – which are not necessarily different across contracts – than do vertically integrated stations. Moreover, this difference is increasing in economic and statistical significance as the endogeneity of the contract choice is more explicitly controlled for, though it never reaches the differences shown by a naive comparison of means. In addition, the results are robust to variation in empirical specification. In particular, although not shown here, the findings remain qualitatively the same when I control for brand-state-date heterogeneity or include county-date effects. Details on models not presented here are available upon request.

5.3 Volume Results

Table 7 presents the results of total volume of fuel sold regressions for the cross-sectional, Mundlak, and two IV models for both a dichotomous indicator variable and individual contract indicator variables.

When vertical separation is modeled using a dichotomous variable, I consistently find that it is associated with lower volumes of fuel sold. These effects generally are economically large and statistically significant, suggesting that as a result of their higher prices vertically separated stations sell lower volumes to consumers with downward sloping demand curves. The lone exception is in column 4, where the effect is not statistically significant and of smaller magnitude.

The story remains largely the same when I switch to controlling for contract choice using individual indicator variables for each contract. As before, I consistently find negative and significant effects on the volume of fuel sold. However, the results are interesting, because they consistently show that stations operated under different contracts sell different volumes of fuel. These differences are statistically significant at conventional levels in all models. As a robustness check that the differences are not being driven by some correlation between organizational form and diesel sales, I estimated models with categorical variables for the different types of diesel sales that New Image identifies. These controls do not have a qualitative impact. Therefore, it seems unlikely that the reason that the coefficients on the different contract types differ is a function of the generality of the dependent variable. Instead, the results imply that the different vertically separated contracts lead to different sales volumes.

That I uncover similar price effects yet dissimilar volume effects across the arms-length forms is consistent with the idea that the price increase from vertical separation is due to different demand-shifting and double marginalization effects and that the relative magnitudes of these effects vary across contracts. In particular, the results suggest that lessee dealers exert greater effort than open dealers or jobber managers, as they sell significantly larger volumes of fuel. One possible explanation may be that lessee dealers are – on average – able to procure their gasoline at lower rates from the

28

dealer tank wagon than open dealers or jobbers. Thus, their profit margin is higher, encouraging them to exert greater effort. This story, however, runs contrary to some anecdotal evidence, which suggests that lessee dealers feel that they are paying *higher* rates than open dealers. On the other hand, the lessee dealers who made these complaints may have done so in part because such a situation represented an inversion of the normal status. I hope to investigate these issues further in future work.

As before, the coefficients on the controls are sometimes statistically insignificant but of generally intuitive signs and magnitudes. The presence of a convenience store is consistently associated with higher sales volumes, though the presence of service bays reduces volume sold. Both findings are consistent with intuition about demand complementarities (positive and negative) among the different products. Similarly, attractive stations sell larger volumes of gasoline, as do those with more nozzles. The number of competitors has negative effects on the volume of sales. Finally, higher incomes are associated with greater sales, while population's impact is weakly negative. As with the price regressions, the model results are robust to less parsimonious sets of controls for regional and temporal variation.

6   Conclusion

A rich literature maps local market and transaction characteristics to the choice of contractual form. However, far fewer papers have attempted to document the impact of these form choices on economic behavior. The reason for this surprising absence is the inherent difficulty of disentangling the impact of form from its determinants. I contribute to the emerging literature that addresses this gap by exploiting unique data on gasoline stations operating in Denver, Minneapolis, Toledo, Louisville, and Washington, DC metropolitan areas. These data provide information on economic behavior, contractual form, and station characteristics, making it possible to deal with the simultaneity of form decisions and economic outcomes.

Using a range of econometric specifications and controlling for the endogeneity of the form decision, I uncover robust evidence of significant price differences between salaried operations (i.e., vertical integration) and the various arms-length organizational forms. Moreover, the magnitude of the price increases I find between vertically integrated salaried operations and all arms-length contracts are smaller but broadly in line with previous work utilizing divorcement laws to identify the impact of organizational form. The difference between my work and this prior literature is consistent with arguments about the downside of identifying marginal effects off of sweeping policy changes that will impact inframarginal as well as marginal stations.

In addition, although I cannot separately identify the magnitude of the double marginalization and demand-shifting effects on price, I find some evidence suggesting the existence of both impacts by examining the evidence of form on sales volume. The results suggest that a greater amount of the price increase at lessee dealer stations is due to demand-shifting relative to the other arms-length forms, because those stations sell larger volumes of gas despite a similar markup in price. Thus, my results suggest that at least some of the higher prices associated with vertical separation reflects the impact of demand shifting, complicating welfare analysis.

Overall, the paper's results should be of interest not just to scholars but also policy-makers and practitioners. Many refiners are making the decision to get out of direct operation of retail gasoline stations (MSNBC, 2008). Holding all else constant, this paper's analysis suggests that such structural changes could significantly affect pricing and other product market considerations.

References

Barron, J.M. and J.R. Umbeck, "Effects of Different Contractual Arrangements: The Case of Retail Gasoline Markets," *Journal of Law and Economics*, 1984, *27*, 313–328.

Blair, R.D. and F. Lafontaine, *The Economics of Franchising*, Cambridge University Press, 2005.

Blass, A.A. and D.W. Carlton, "Choice of Organization Form in Gasoline Retailing and the Cost of Laws That Limit That Choice," *Journal of Law and Economics*, 2001, *44*, 511–524.

Brickley, J.A., "Incentive Conflicts and Contractual Restraints: Evidence from Franchising," *Journal of Law & Economics*, 1999, *42* (2), 745–74.

_ and F.H. Dark, "The choice of organizational form The case of franchising," *Journal of Financial Economics*, 1987, *18* (2), 401–420.

Coase, R.H., "The nature of the firm," *Economica*, 1937, pp. 386–405.

Forbes, S.J. and M. Lederman, "Adaptation and vertical integration in the airline industry," *The American Economic Review*, 2009, *99* (5), 1831–1849.

_ and _ , "Does vertical integration affect firm performance? Evidence from the airline industry," *The RAND Journal of Economics*, 2010.

Grossman, S.J. and O.D. Hart, "The costs and benefits of ownership: A theory of vertical and lateral integration," *The Journal of Political Economy*, 1986, *94* (4), 691–719.

Hart, O. and J. Moore, "Property Rights and the Nature of the Firm," *Journal of Political Economy*, 1990, *98* (6), 1119–1158.

Hastings, J.S., "Vertical relationships and competition in retail gasoline markets: Empirical evidence from contract changes in southern California," *American Economic Review*, 2004, *94* (1), 317–328.

Holmstrom, B. and P. Milgrom, "Multitask principal-agent analyses: Incentive contracts, asset ownership, and job design," *Journal of Law, Economics, and Organization*, 1991, *7* (special issue), 24–52.

Hosken, D.S., R.S. McMillan, and C.T. Taylor, "Retail gasoline pricing: What do we know?," *International Journal of Industrial Organization*, 2008, *26* (6), 1425–1436.

Hubbard, T.N., "Viewpoint: Empirical research on firms' boundaries," *Canadian Journal of Economics/Revue canadienne d'économique*, 2008, *41* (2), 341–359.

Jin, G.Z. and P. Leslie, "Reputational incentives for restaurant hygiene," *American Economic Journal: Microeconomics*, 2009, *1* (1), 237–267.

Kalnins, A. and F. Lafontaine, "Multi-unit ownership in franchising: evidence from the fast-food industry in Texas," *RAND Journal of Economics*, 2004, pp. 747–761.

Klein, B., "Transaction cost determinants of "unfair" contractual arrangements," *The American Economic Review*, 1980, *70* (2), 356–362.

_ , "The economics of franchise contracts," *Journal of Corporate Finance*, 1995, *2* (1-2), 9–37.

Kleit, A.N., "The Economics of Gasoline Retailing: Petroleum Distribution and Retailing Issues in the U. S," *Energy Studies Review*, 2005, *13* (2), 1–28.

Kosova, R., F. Lafontaine, and R. Perrigot, "Organizational Form and Performance: Evidence from the Hotel Industry," *Cornell University, mimeo*, 2010.

Laffont, J.J. and D. Martimort, *The theory of incentives: the principal-agent model*, Princeton Univ Pr, 2002.

Lafontaine, F. and M. Slade, "Retail contracting and costly monitoring: Theory and evidence," *European Economic Review*, 1996, *40* (3-5), 923–932.

_ **and** _ , "Vertical integration and firm boundaries: the evidence," *Journal of Economic Literature*, 2007, *45* (3), 629–685.

_ **and** _ , "Inter-Firm Contracts: Evidence," in R. Gibbons and J. Roberts, eds., *Handbook of Organizational Economics*, Princeton University Press, Princeton, 2011.

_ , **R. Perrigot, and N.E. Wilson**, "Institutional Quality and Organizational Form Decisions: Evidence from Within the Firm," *working paper*, 2011.

Lal, R. and C. Matutes, "Retail pricing and advertising strategies," *The Journal of Business*, 1994, *67* (3), 345–370.

Masten, S.E., J.W. Meehan Jr, and E.A. Snyder, "The Costs of Organization," *Journal of Law, Economics, and Organization*, 1991, *7* (1), 1–25.

Meyer, D. and J. Fischer, "The Economics of Price Zones and Territorial Restrictions in Gasoline Marketing," *Federal Trade Commission Bureau of Economics Working Paper*, 2004, *271*.

Michael, S.C., "The effect of organizational form on quality: the case of franchising," *Journal of Economic Behavior & Organization*, 2000, *43* (3), 295–318.

MSNBC, "Exxon to sell all of companys gas stations," *MSNBC.com*, 2008.

Mullainathan, S. and D. Scharfstein, "Do firm boundaries matter?," *American Economic Review*, 2001, *91* (2), 195–199.

Mundlak, Y., "On the pooling of time series and cross section data," *Econometrica*, 1978, pp. 69–85.

Novak, S. and S. Stern, "How does outsourcing affect performance dynamics? Evidence from the automobile industry," *Management Science*, 2008, *54* (12), 1963–1979.

_ **and** _ , "Complementarity among vertical integration decisions: evidence from automobile product development," *Management Science*, 2009, *55* (2), 311–332.

Perez-Gonzalez, F., "The impact of acquiring control on productivity," *Stanford University, mimeo*, 2005.

Shelton, J.P., "Allocative Efficiency vs. 'X-Efficiency': Comment," *The American Economic Review*, 1967, *57* (5), 1252–1258.

Shepard, A., "Contractual form, retail price, and asset characteristics in gasoline retailing," *RAND Journal of Economics*, 1993, *24* (1), 58–77.

Slade, M.E., "Multitask agency and contract choice: an empirical exploration," *International Economic Review*, 1996, *37* (2), 465–486.

Spengler, J.J., "Vertical integration and antitrust policy," *The Journal of Political Economy*, 1950, pp. 347–352.

Taylor, C.T., N.M. Kreisle, and P.R. Zimmerman, "Vertical Relationships and Competition in Retail Gasoline Markets: Empirical Evidence from Contract Changes in Southern California: Comment," *The American Economic Review*, 2010, *100* (3), 1269–1276.

Vita, M.G., "Regulatory restrictions on vertical integration and control: The competitive impact of gasoline divorcement policies," *Journal of Regulatory Economics*, 2000, *18* (3), 217–233.

Williamson, O.E., *Markets and hierarchies, analysis and antitrust implications: a study in the economics of internal organization*, Free Press New York, 1975.

Wilson, N.E., "Local Market Structure and Strategic Organizational Form Choices: Evidence from Gasoline Stations," *working paper*, 2011.

Wooldridge, J.M., *Econometric analysis of cross section and panel data*, The MIT press, 2002.

Table 1: Descriptive Statistics

Variable	Obs	Mean	Std. Dev.	Min	Max
Regular	4299	116.71	13.73	79.90	167.90
Super	4296	126.70	13.15	86.90	186.90
Premium	4299	134.86	12.52	88.90	193.90
Volume	4535	104.99	50.32	10.00	400.00
Competitors	4687	10.89	7.43	0.00	38.00
1(C-Store)	4687	0.72	0.45	0.00	1.00
1(Service Bays)	4687	0.39	0.49	0.00	1.00
1(Appearance)	4687	0.15	0.35	0.00	1.00
Nozzles	4535	18.13	9.95	2.00	60.00
Pop. ('000s)	4687	619.02	294.32	40.99	1109.63
Income ('000s)	4687	57.87	14.59	35.47	96.69

Table 2: Descriptive Statistics Across Vertically Integrated and Separated Stations

	Integrated			Separated			
Variable	Obs	Mean	Std. Dev.	Obs	Mean	Std. Dev.	T-Stat
Variable	Obs	Mean	Std. Dev.	Obs	Mean	Std. Dev.	T-Stat
Regular	657	106.63	16.37	3642	118.53	12.36	-70.74
Super	657	117.86	14.70	3639	128.29	12.19	-65.06
Premium	657	127.03	14.11	3642	136.28	11.66	-58.88
Volume	671	138.63	51.25	3864	99.15	47.81	132.53
Competitors	823	11.78	8.65	3864	10.70	7.14	9.66
1(C-Store)	823	0.67	0.47	3864	0.73	0.45	-2.34
1(Service Bays)	823	0.06	0.24	3864	0.46	0.50	-19.71
1(Appearance)	823	0.25	0.43	3864	0.13	0.33	4.81
Nozzles	671	20.13	10.91	3864	17.79	9.73	17.07
Pop. ('000s)	823	545.48	274.94	3864	634.68	295.96	-139.20
Income ('000s)	823	59.21	14.55	3864	57.59	14.59	11.07

Table 3: Descriptive Statistics Across Vertically Separated Contracts

Variable	Lessee			Open			Jobber			L vs. O	L vs. J	O vs. J
	Obs	Mean	Std. Dev.	Obs	Mean	Std. Dev.	Obs	Mean	Std. Dev.	T-Stat	T-Stat	T-Stat
Regular	1718	119.97	10.80	1012	118.82	12.76	912	115.50	14.03	2.41	15.76	8.82
Medium	1718	130.82	10.55	1009	127.56	12.81	912	124.34	13.19	6.84	25.35	9.10
Premium	1718	137.85	10.17	1012	136.36	12.24	912	133.23	12.98	3.26	18.85	9.40
Volume	1763	124.64	42.79	1082	65.95	34.84	1019	90.29	42.92	39.94	12.07	-8.31
Competitors	1763	10.52	6.36	1082	10.29	7.61	1019	11.45	7.80	0.83	-11.22	-10.23
1(C-Store)	1763	0.76	0.43	1082	0.60	0.49	1019	0.81	0.39	8.53	-202.61	-551.61
1(Service Bays)	1763	0.60	0.49	1082	0.60	0.49	1019	0.09	0.28	-0.12	2367.17	1702.52
1(Appearance)	1763	0.16	0.37	1082	0.06	0.24	1019	0.14	0.35	8.92	95.36	-481.40
Nozzles	1763	22.44	8.98	1082	12.02	7.57	1019	15.86	9.08	33.17	51.98	-28.71
Pop. ('000s)	1763	718.38	255.69	1082	596.80	317.15	1019	530.10	296.34	10.66	1.53	0.37
Income ('000s)	1763	60.77	15.25	1082	56.85	14.70	1019	52.87	11.62	6.81	29.88	11.98

Table 4: The Price of Regular Unleaded and Vertical Contracting

	OLS b/se	Mundlak b/se	IV b/se	IV Mundlak b/se	OLS b/se	Mundlak b/se	IV b/se	IV Mundlak b/se
Separated	0.291	1.236***	3.482***	5.211***				
	0.28	0.38	1.09	1.74				
Lessee					0.496*	1.125***	2.688***	4.191***
					[0.295]	[0.350]	[0.964]	[1.579]
Open					0.689*	1.103**	3.753***	4.704
					[0.361]	[0.447]	[1.212]	[3.289]
Jobber					-0.306	0.654	1.807**	5.327**
					[0.328]	[0.546]	[0.863]	[2.195]
Competition	-0.071***	-0.074	-0.069***	-0.079	-0.071***	-0.07	-0.068***	-0.08
	0.02	0.06	0.02	0.07	[0.020]	[0.064]	[0.020]	[0.064]
C-Store	-0.702***	-0.29	-0.796***	-0.528**	-0.640***	-0.326	-0.552**	-0.477
	0.21	0.25	0.21	0.25	[0.202]	[0.251]	[0.217]	[0.328]
Service Bays	0.674***	0.493*	0.365*	0.224	0.426**	0.39	0.044	0.419
	0.19	0.25	0.22	0.28	[0.201]	[0.268]	[0.301]	[0.375]
Appearance	-0.282+	-0.855***	0.071	-0.727**	-0.294	-0.892***	-0.007	-0.798**
	0.18	0.3	0.22	0.32	[0.183]	[0.292]	[0.224]	[0.319]
Population	0	-0.009	0	-0.026	0	-0.019	0	-0.027
	0	0.03	0	0.03	[0.001]	[0.030]	[0.001]	[0.033]
Income	0.098***	0.026	0.097***	0.025	0.098***	0.028	0.101***	0.034
	0.01	0.09	0.01	0.09	[0.014]	[0.086]	[0.013]	[0.084]
Lag Volume	0.007	0.007	0.006	0.006		0.008		0.006
	0.01	0.01	0.01	0.01		[0.011]		[0.011]
State-Date Effects	Yes	Yes	Yes	Yes	Yes	Yes	Yes	Yes
Brand Effects	Yes	Yes	Yes	Yes	Yes	Yes	Yes	Yes
Observations	4299	1616	4298	1615	4,298	1,615	4,263	1,604
Equivalent	0.001				0.001	0.497	0.092	0.654
F Separated			72.196	18.515				
F Type LD							102.223	42.931
F Type OD							62.21	5.33
F Type WJ							164.817	16.795

* p<0.10, ** p<0.05, *** p<0.01. Notes: "Equivalent" provides the p-value of a χ^2 test that the coefficients on the different contractual forms are equal. Mundlak models all contain means of lagged volume, number of competitors, population, and income.

36

Table 5: The Price of Super Unleaded and Vertical Contracting

	OLS	Mundlak	IV	IV Mundlak	OLS	Mundlak	IV	IV Mundlak
	b/se	b/se	b/se	b/se	b/se	b/se	b/se	b/se
Separated	0.174	2.080***	0.457	8.365***				
	0.37	0.54	1.41	2.25				
Lessee					0.657*	1.896***	1.879	6.367***
					[0.371]	[0.492]	[1.252]	[1.919]
Open					0.031	1.752***	-0.091	6.386*
					[0.460]	[0.596]	[1.673]	[3.809]
Jobber					-0.627	1.256*	-0.957	7.407***
					[0.475]	[0.668]	[1.323]	[2.610]
Competition	-0.051**	0.014	-0.051**	0.007	-0.053**	0.022	-0.057**	0.009
	0.02	0.09	0.02	0.09	[0.024]	[0.086]	[0.024]	[0.086]
C-Store	0.041	-0.141	-0.01	-0.518+	-0.022	-0.218	-0.15	-0.496
	0.31	0.31	0.31	0.32	[0.306]	[0.306]	[0.332]	[0.396]
Service Bays	1.076***	0.560*	1.025***	0.135	0.871***	0.426	0.714*	0.43
	0.27	0.32	0.29	0.35	[0.281]	[0.324]	[0.419]	[0.451]
Appearance	0.284	-0.881**	0.29	-0.678+	0.228	-0.933**	0.209	-0.760*
	0.23	0.41	0.26	0.46	[0.225]	[0.404]	[0.272]	[0.446]
Population	0	-0.039	0	-0.066**	0	-0.055**	0	-0.069**
	0	0.03	0	0.03	[0.001]	[0.028]	[0.001]	[0.032]
Income	0.137***	0.186*	0.137***	0.184*	0.138***	0.190*	0.141***	0.195*
	0.02	0.1	0.02	0.1	[0.017]	[0.104]	[0.017]	[0.101]
Lag Volume	-0.005	-0.005	-0.005	-0.006		-0.003		-0.006
	0.01	0.01	0.01	0.01		[0.014]		[0.014]
State-Date Effects	Yes	Yes	Yes	Yes	Yes	Yes	Yes	Yes
Brand Effects	Yes	Yes	Yes	Yes	Yes	Yes	Yes	Yes
Observations	4296	1616	4295	1615	4,295	1,615	4,260	1,604
Equivalent					0.016	0.432	0.019	0.743
F Separated			71.987	18.515				
F Type LD							102.204	42.931
F Type OD							62.195	5.33
F Type WJ							164.319	16.795

* p<0.10, ** p<0.05, *** p<0.01. Notes: "Equivalent" provides the p-value of a χ^2 test that the coefficients on the different contractual forms are equal. Mundlak models all contain means of lagged volume, number of competitors, population, and income.

Table 6: The Price of Premium Unleaded and Vertical Contracting

	OLS b/se	Mundlak b/se	IV b/se	IV Mundlak b/se	OLS b/se	Mundlak b/se	IV b/se	IV Mundlak b/se
Separated	0.171	2.120***	1.864	7.076***				
	0.39	0.6	1.53	2.36				
Lessee					0.566	1.807***	1.123	5.503**
					[0.403]	[0.525]	[1.295]	[2.181]
Open					0.579	2.067***	0.848	4.401
					[0.468]	[0.649]	[1.721]	[4.389]
Jobber					-0.816*	1.929**	-0.275	7.438**
					[0.486]	[0.753]	[1.366]	[3.037]
Competition	-0.064**	0.043	-0.063**	0.041	-0.064**	0.054	-0.065**	0.047
	0.03	0.1	0.03	0.1	[0.028]	[0.096]	[0.028]	[0.097]
C-Store	-0.400+	-0.236	-0.491*	-0.580+	-0.355	-0.327	-0.403	-0.748
	0.3	0.37	0.29	0.35	[0.290]	[0.362]	[0.312]	[0.459]
Service Bays	1.185***	0.722**	0.998***	0.355	0.821***	0.639*	0.874**	0.892*
	0.27	0.34	0.31	0.35	[0.279]	[0.357]	[0.414]	[0.499]
Appearance	-0.071	-0.788+	0.093	-0.650+	-0.109	-0.873*	-0.066	-0.635
	0.26	0.48	0.3	0.5	[0.259]	[0.471]	[0.303]	[0.511]
Population	0	0.035	0	0.007	0	0.018	0	-0.004
	0	0.04	0	0.04	[0.001]	[0.035]	[0.001]	[0.038]
Income	0.155***	0.061	0.155***	0.064	0.156***	0.075	0.159***	0.082
	0.02	0.11	0.02	0.11	[0.020]	[0.110]	[0.019]	[0.111]
Lag Volume		0.004		0.003		0.005		0.005
		0.02		0.02		[0.016]		[0.016]
State-Date Effects	Yes	Yes	Yes	Yes	Yes	Yes	Yes	Yes
Brand Effects	Yes	Yes	Yes	Yes	Yes	Yes	Yes	Yes
Observations	4299	1616	4298	1615	4,298	1,615	4,263	1,604
Equivalent	0				0	0.846	0.405	0.355
F Separated			72.196	18.515				
F Type LD							102.223	42.931
F Type OD							62.21	5.33
F Type WJ							164.817	16.795

* p<0.10, ** p<0.05, *** p<0.01. Notes: "Equivalent" provides the p-value of a χ^2 test that the coefficients on the different contractual forms are equal. Mundlak models all contain means of lagged volume, number of competitors, population, and income.

Table 7: Volume of Sales and Vertical Contracting

	OLS b/se	Mundlak b/se	IV b/se	IV Mundlak b/se	OLS b/se	Mundlak b/se	IV b/se	IV Mundlak b/se
Separated	-28.929*** [3.648]	-24.228*** [6.187]	-31.634*** [8.116]	-11.726 [17.408]				
Lessee					-20.845*** [3.974]	-21.524*** [6.025]	-20.388** [10.055]	-6.395 [18.443]
Open					-46.017*** [3.701]	-45.142*** [6.970]	-39.084** [17.748]	-8.818 [41.868]
Jobber					-34.396*** [3.369]	-36.814*** [7.858]	-42.640*** [9.228]	-48.151* [28.867]
Competition	-0.216* [0.114]	0.828 [0.664]	-0.218* [0.112]	0.807 [0.653]	-0.269** [0.106]	0.761 [0.663]	-0.265** [0.112]	0.822 [0.702]
C-Store	3.962** [1.950]	5.134* [2.962]	4.043** [1.963]	4.61 [2.972]	1.007 [1.812]	2.74 [2.789]	2.538 [2.071]	4.919 [4.122]
Service Bays	-10.682*** [1.712]	-14.293*** [2.758]	-10.449*** [1.862]	-15.275*** [3.119]	-9.054*** [1.809]	-13.090*** [2.755]	-12.266*** [3.424]	-20.215*** [5.821]
Appearance	22.584*** [2.216]	17.803*** [5.128]	22.288*** [2.377]	18.843*** [5.075]	21.815*** [2.168]	17.984*** [4.923]	21.836*** [2.657]	17.393*** [5.118]
Nozzles	2.601*** [0.094]	2.513*** [0.160]	2.590*** [0.099]	2.574*** [0.178]	2.409*** [0.095]	2.320*** [0.167]	2.474*** [0.151]	2.644*** [0.362]
Population	0.007** [0.003]	-0.088 [0.331]	0.007** [0.003]	-0.111 [0.310]	0.004 [0.003]	-0.235 [0.313]	0.003 [0.003]	-0.103 [0.282]
Income	-0.047 [0.085]	1.278* [0.652]	-0.047 [0.084]	1.254** [0.624]	-0.052 [0.081]	1.088* [0.632]	-0.039 [0.082]	0.789 [0.653]
Lag Price		0.658 [0.519]		0.653 [0.507]		0.67 [0.551]		0.459 [0.561]
Observation	4,298	1,383	4,298	1,383	4,298	1,383	4,263	1,378
Equivalent	0				0	0	0	0.099
F Separated			101.654	36.363				
F Type LD							117.736	30.7
F Type OD							45.241	5.013
F Type WJ							219.572	7.172

* $p<0.10$, ** $p<0.05$, *** $p<0.01$. Notes: "Equivalent" provides the p-value of a χ^2 test that the coefficients on the different contractual forms are equal. Mundlak models all contain means of lagged regular price, number of competitors, population, and income.

Appendix A: Proofs of Propositions

PROPOSITION 1: *Conditional on an arms-length contractual form being chosen in equilibrium for an station, its prices will on average be higher than if it was operated as a salaried operation.*

PROOF:
In order for prices under vertical separation to be higher than under vertical integration, then:

$$p_1^{S*} = \frac{a_1 - p_2(2b_{12} - \tilde{c_{12}} + r\sigma_{12}) + \sigma_{11}r\alpha}{2b_{11} - \tilde{c_{11}} + r\sigma_{11}} > \frac{a_1 - 2b_{12}p_2}{2b_{11}} = p_1^{I*}. \tag{15}$$

The point of using an arms-length contract is to induce additional effort on the part of the agent relative to what they would exert under vertical integration ($e = 0$). And the inverse demand function implied by Equation 1 shows that $e > 0$ will lead to higher prices on average. Thus, in the region of the parameter space where an arms-length contract would be selected, prices on average will exceed those if the same station was operated under vertical integration.

COROLLARY 1: *This price increase can be decomposed into two separate influences: i) Double marginalization; and ii) Demand-shifting. Moreover, even in the absence of double marginalization, the demand-shifting effect will lead – on average – to higher prices at stations operated under high-powered contracts.*

PROOF: This can be shown to be true by separating out the linearly entering term containing α. Thus, :

$$
\begin{aligned}
0 \quad &< \quad \frac{a_1 - p_2(2b_{12} - \tilde{c_{12}} + r\sigma_{12}) + \sigma_{11}r\alpha}{2b_{11} - \tilde{c_{11}} + r\sigma_{11}} - \frac{a_1 - 2b_{12}p_2}{2b_{11}} \\
&< \quad \left(\frac{a_1 - p_2(2b_{12} - \tilde{c_{12}} + r\sigma_{12})}{2b_{11} - \tilde{c_{11}} + r\sigma_{11}} - \frac{a_1 - 2b_{12}p_2}{2b_{11}} \right) + \frac{\sigma_{11}r\alpha}{2b_{11} - \tilde{c_{11}} + r\sigma_{11}}. \tag{16}
\end{aligned}
$$

Thus, even if the principal sets $\alpha = 0$, the first term still causes prices at vertically integrated to be on average higher than they would be under integration – conditional on the fact that the firm did choose to operate the station using an arms-length contract.

PROPOSITION 2: *The factors that lead to a larger demand-shifting effect on prices also increase the desirability of using an arms-length contract.*

PROOF:
This can be neatly shown by differentiating Equations 9 and 11 with respect to the various model parameters. Then, by applying the envelope theorem and assumptions about the signs of the different it can be shown that the same parameters increasing the effort-induced term in 16 also increase the payoff of using vertical separation.

Appendix B: New Image Data Description

Below, I provide the name and description provided by New Image of those variables used in the analysis and the method by which they were transformed (if appropriate).

- Organizational Form: Categorical variable corresponding to the answer to the following question. TYPE OF OPERATION)(TOO) - Overall status of operation, ask respondent to identify:
  0) - No building or doesn't sell gasoline
  1) - Lessee dealer building and facility owned by major/non major oil company, business owned by dealer. [I reordered this as Type 2.]
  2) - Salary operation building and facility owned by major/non major oil company. Personnel paid

by company. [I reordered this as Type 1, so that salaried operations represented the baseline.]

3) - Open Dealer - Land and operation owned by individual who is supplied product by major/non major oil company.

4) - Jobber/Wholesaler Operation owned by a local company that owns several operations in the area. (EXP distributor) or a franchise/chain organization (EXP a convenience store chain)

- Regular Unleaded Price: Numerical variable corresponding to non-constrained answer to the following question. OCT REGULAR UNLEADED)(UO) - Price Reg Unleaded)(RUP)

- Super Unleaded Price: Numerical variable corresponding to non-constrained answer to the following question. OCT MIDGRADE UNLEADED)(MO) - Price mid Unleaded)(MUP)

- Premium Unleaded Price: Numerical variable corresponding to non-constrained answer to the following question. OCT SUPER)(SO) - Price Super Unleaded)(PUP)

- Volume: Numerical variable corresponding to non-constrained answer to the following question. MONTHLY VOLUME)(GV) - Enter average number of gallons sold in one month. (last completed month)

- C-Store: Dummy variable which takes value of 1 if an answer other than 0 chosen for the following question. INTERIOR C-STORE APPEARANCE)(INAP) As it appears to consumer.
  0) - No snack shop
  1) - Outstanding (top 102) - Excellent
  3) - Better than average
  4) - Equal to average
  5) - Below average
  6) - Poor
  7) - Unacceptable (bottom 10

- Service Bays: Dummy variable which takes value of 1 if a number other than 0 chosen for the following question. SERVICE BAYS)(NOSB) - Total number of service bays. If not in operation mention in comments.

- Appearance: Dummy variable which takes value of 1 if the answer to the following question takes the value of 1 or 2. APPEARANCE OF BUILDING)(AOB) -
  0) - N/A
  1) - Outstanding (top 10%)
  2) - Excellent
  3) - Better than average
  4) - Equal to average
  5) - Below average
  6) - poor
  7) - Unacceptable (bottom 10%)

- Nozzles: Numerical variable corresponding to non-constrained answer to the following question. GASOLINE NOZZLES)(GN) - Total number of gasoline only nozzles. Do not include diesel or kerosene.

Appendix C: Additional Tables

Table C-1: Station-Period Observations by State and Year

	1996	1997	1998	1999	2000	Total
CO	0	0	0	630	0	630
	0	*0*	*0*	*100*	*0*	*100*
DC	0	117	0	109	0	226
	0	*51.77*	*0*	*48.23*	*0*	*100*
KY	239	237	0	244	0	720
	33.19	*32.92*	*0*	*33.89*	*0*	*100*
MD	0	437	0	444	0	881
	0	*49.6*	*0*	*50.4*	*0*	*100*
MN	0	0	0	600	0	600
	0	*0*	*0*	*100*	*0*	*100*
OH	0	0	0	0	185	185
	0	*0*	*0*	*0*	*100*	*100*
VA	0	478	482	485	0	1,445
	0	*33.08*	*33.36*	*33.56*	*0*	*100*
Total	239	1,269	482	2,512	185	4,687
	5.1	*27.07*	*10.28*	*53.6*	*3.95*	*100*

Rows in *italics* represent percentages.

Table C-2: Station-Period Observations by State and Form

	Company Owned	Lessee Dealer	Open Dealer	Jobber	Total
CO	290	57	99	184	630
	46.03	*9.05*	*15.71*	*29.21*	*100*
DC	0	154	43	2	199
	0	*77.39*	*21.61*	*1.01*	*100*
KY	49	74	233	364	720
	6.81	*10.28*	*32.36*	*50.56*	*100*
MD	14	619	157	44	834
	1.68	*74.22*	*18.82*	*5.28*	*100*
MN	57	95	198	250	600
	9.5	*15.83*	*33*	*41.67*	*100*
OH	70	15	45	55	185
	37.84	*8.11*	*24.32*	*29.73*	*100*
VA	191	749	307	120	1,367
	13.97	*54.79*	*22.46*	*8.78*	*100*
Total	671	1,763	1,082	1,019	4,535
	14.8	*38.88*	*23.86*	*22.47*	*100*

Rows in *italics* represent percentages.

Table C-3: First Stage of Mundlak Instrumental Variables Price Model

	Type = 2 b/se	Type = 3 b/se	Type = 4 b/se
Share Type 2	0.774***	-0.173**	-0.012
	0.087	0.075	0.051
Share Type 3	0.145	0.181	0.199**
	0.117	0.111	0.094
Share Type 4	-0.046	-0.148	0.699***
	0.101	0.114	0.105
Nozzles	0.001	-0.003**	0.001
	0.002	0.001	0.001
Competitors	-0.001	0.004	-0.003
	0.005	0.006	0.004
C-Store	0.080***	-0.106***	0.048***
	0.027	0.027	0.018
Service Bays	0.072**	0.115***	-0.130***
	0.028	0.024	0.018
Appearance	-0.089**	0.040	0.011
	0.037	0.028	0.020
Population	0.007*	-0.005***	0.001
	0.004	0.002	0.002
Income	-0.003	0.002	-0.004
	0.007	0.007	0.006
Lag Volume	-0.001	0.001	0.000
	0.001	0.001	0.000
Brand Effects	Yes	Yes	Yes
State-Date Effects	Yes	Yes	Yes
Observations	1604	1604	1604

* $p<0.10$, ** $p<0.05$, *** $p<0.01$.

44

www.ingramcontent.com/pod-product-compliance
Lightning Source LLC
Chambersburg PA
CBHW081237170526
45165CB00009B/3090